THROUGH MY EYES

ARTWORK BY
DONA ROUSSEAU
&
DANIEL TABAKA

POETRY BY
CURT SOWULO

CLOSE THE LOOP
PO BOX 748
SCAPPOOSE, OR 97056-0748

Through My Eyes

Close The Loop,

an Oregon Publishing Company

P.O. Box 748

Scappoose, Oregon 97056-0748

This publication is dedicated
to those of you who will take a journey with us
and chronicle your hopes and dreams on these pages.

Table of Poetry

Imagine a meadow—
Aglow in early morning light,
Suggesting the warmth to come.
Imagine lush green grasses—
Eagerly reaching for the sun.
Imagine clovers and buttercups—
Deer nibbling on tender shoots.
Imagine wonderful little creatures
Traveling tiny paths—
Industrious ants, beetles, spiders—
Others too numerous to tally.
Imagine mice, voles—
Busy foraging for nourishment.
Imagine snakes, lizards—
Lazing in the sun.
Imagine robins, meadowlarks—
Singing their simple arias.
Imagine a gentle breeze—
Freshing the air.
Imagine a sky—cobalt blue—
Golden sunlight dazzling the eye.
Imagine such glorious display—
Staggering the mind
With the wonders of life.
Imagine me alone
Immersed in magnificence—
With no one to share . . .

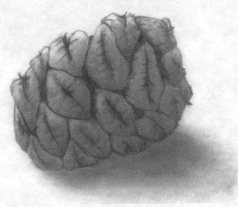

Patience unsurpassed . . .
    Like wind carving mountains.
Watching, waiting for opportunity . . .
    Never a detail missed.
Eyes of the wolf—
    X-ray lenses,
        Piercing, probing, penetrating—
            Exposing each fiber and cell
                Of their chosen prey.
Perception beyond ordinary . . .
Uncanny psychic vision—
    Sensing weakness, disease,
Quiet observation—
    Poised for the strike.

Within my mind—
    Inner eyes probe . . .
        Searching tenaciously for flaws—
        Relentlessly holding beliefs
            Before the light of truth—
            Laying bare its deceptions—
    Ever vigilant . . .
        Like the eyes of the wolf.

I hear a voice in the windsong—
>> It is Red-tail: "I am the messenger of the sky.
>>> On my wings I carry the power of vision and perspective.
>>> Soar with me and you will see the path
>>> That will restore your soul."

I hear a voice in the riversong—
>> It is Dragonfly: "I am illusion. In the iridescence of my wings
>>> Are the secrets of magic and perception.
>>> Look closely, with imagination,
>>>> And I will reveal to you the soulfulness of being."

I hear a voice in the song of life—
>> It is Wolf: "I am the teacher of discrimination and persistence;
>>> On the hunt, my eyes see truth and my strong legs follow.
>>> Run with me—howl to the moon,
>>>> And know the soulful power of aggression."

I hear a voice in the song of the sea—
>> It is Humpback: "I am the record keeper of Mother Earth;
>>> In my songs are the memories of ancient knowledge.
>>> Listen carefully and remember the truth
>>>> That will quiet your soul-searching.

I hear voices in the Earthsong—
>> "We, the creatures and substance of the Cosmos,
>>> Are a community of One—
>>> Each unique in purpose and form
>>>> Yet One in essence

As the seas, clouds, and rains.
>> Together, we walk the Dreamtime.

Lying in sun-drenched meadow . . .

Hint of dampness under back—

Sun's glow and warmth

Reaching deep inside with healing touch—

Luxuriating in pungent smells of humus.

Sweet incense of lilacs

Hovering near, then fading—

 Tickling, teasing my nose,

  Flitting about it like a butterfly.

Daydreaming, pondering the boundaries

Between imagination and reality—

Thoughts wandering—

Intoxicated by the input of my senses.

Closing my eyes . . .

I grasp a tulip–

 With deep breath, inhaling its beauty

 And, touching delicate petals to lips—

  Drink my fill,

 Satiating my soul with a

  Sweet elixir of life.

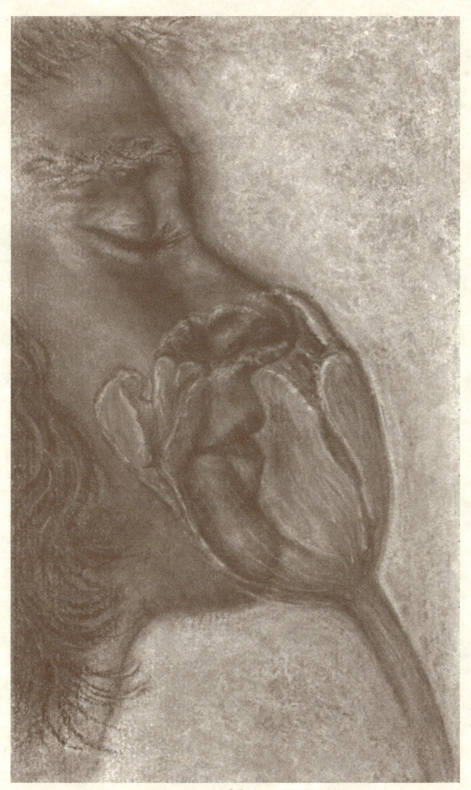

Still, sure power of a golden eagle—
Circles . . . rises . . . slowly on warming air—
  Breath of God
  Whispers through jack pine.
Crystal voices of meadowlarks,
  Red-winged blackbirds . . .
Gregorian chants of crickets, bullfrogs . . .
Staccato splashes of rainbow trout, painted turtles—
  Circles within circles
  On peaceful waters.
Dissonant accents of
  Brassy Indian paintbrush,
  Dulcet Western larkspur.
Glow of sunlight,
  Circadian harmony,
   Restores the spirit.
Summer's living symphony
  Touches the soul softly as
   Morning dew on rye-grass—
  Brings peace to all who listen.
Raise then your voice—
Join her spontaneous refrain—
  Celebrate the beauty.

Up there!
Suspended high
     In black velvet sky,
The mother of wisdom—
Always changing
     Yet ever the same—
Shares borrowed rays
     Without favor
To all below.
And what lies hidden
     'Neath her ephemeral glow
          And its shadows,
But a world that slumbers—
     Yet never sleeps.

For the nocturnes—
     Unhurried,
In shadowland,
Dwell unaffected—
     Still of spirit, accepting.
Permeating the mists
     Of primeval forests,
          Thundering cataracts,
The Mother's gift
     Is honored—
Not by accomplishment
     Nor by understanding,
But in being.
Look beyond and between,
Escaping the vanity of knowing
And find within—
     That which never changes . . . .
Her wisdom.

I will learn to hear—
    Special beauty in each minute rainbow
    As sunbeams refract through dewdrops.
    Morning mists lingering over lush meadows.
I will learn to see—
    Songs of winged creatures—and whales.
    Sweetness in vine-ripened fruits.
I will learn to taste—
    Beauty of a star-lit night.
    Fragrance of a rose.
I will learn to touch—
    Stealth of an owl—the hunter.
    Fear of a mouse—the hunted.
I will learn to smell—
    Crunching footsteps in fresh snow.
    Moon's pull on ocean tides.

I must let go of perceptions past
    That instill feelings of limitations—
        And hold me captive.

Soaring...
Gliding high upon breath of God.
Wings outstretched—
Each feather grasping for lift.
Tail feathers turned at sharp angles—
Cutting circles in a cobalt sky.
Eyes alert, piercing...
Watching below—
Seeing every movement.
Patience . . .
Opportunity—an unwary vole—
Action without hesitation,
Wings fold—
Plummeting to earth,
Talons outstretched,
Grabbing, clutching prey.
Transference—
In one instant...
Life and death.

I see rolling prairies and open spaces—
Bright sunlit azure skies with downy traces
  Of someday's rain over miles of green.
Life in process.
I smell the marriage of the sun's energy,
With Earth's life-giving waters and minerals
   Lingering in the air—sweet, pungent, musky—
    And know in my whole being—
    The promise of its potential.
With both feet grounded solidly on ancient loam,
My spirit mounts the breeze and soars
   Far and wide upon the currents of my imagination.
I am utterly and joyously alone in my communion with nature
   And yet ever more aware of my connections to all.
As night falls and cool moonglow settles over the land,
   Stealing away colors, dropping an ethereal veil
   Of darkness over sensory perceptions—
My imagination, stirred to urgency by night's reins,
Springs forth with bursts of brief intensity
   Like the flash of dying embers stirred one last time
   Before being quenched.
With heightened awareness,
I feel the deep, slow rhythms of Earth's sleep-breath,
Drawing the stress of daytime obligations out of my breast—
Inhaling, exhaling, joining Earth's rhythms with my own.
I am at peace with myself and my world,
Ready to lie down and enter the realm of dreams
   Where my spirit recognizes not the limitations
   Imposed by the perceptions of physical boundaries.
Life in process.

Dawn . . .
Petal soft, rose-colored skies—
  Stillness permeates the air.
Creation, bathed in hush of expectancy.
Ethereal mists suspended over glassy pond.
Peering tentatively over hill and vale—
   A golden sun, its radiating glow
    Marks night's passage—
    Stirs nature to life.

Mid-day . . .
Robin's egg skies—bright and warm.
Lush green grasses—
Pungent rainbow of roses, rhododendrons—
Majestic oaks rustle in a cooling breeze.
Everywhere, the bustle of living things—
   Meadowlarks sing arias from perches,
   Squirrels chatter—scolding passers-by.
A solitary figure—
   Sits in the shade of an ancient, gnarled oak,
    Simply drinking it all in—
    Pondering secrets of the cosmos.

Evening . . .
Deer and elk slip out of cover,
Feeding peacefully on shrubs and sweet-grasses.
The sun lingers, then dips below the horizon—
   Glorious hues . . . crimson, umber, magenta.
Shadows soften the edges of vision
   As colors fade to shades of gray.
Frantic flight of bat wings—
   Chase away the last hints of day.

Nightfall . . .
Crickets, frogs sing lullabies.
Sun on moon—nocturnal night-light.
Owls posted at sentry,
Seeing all, call the hour.

The world sleeps.

Clouds drifting lazily across the heavens,
Carriers of life, on a pilgrimage of giving.
Droplets of water falling to the earth—
Rivulets dashing over the ground—
Beginnings of a sojourn to the sea.
Whisper of a gentle mountain brook
Tickles my ears with its sweet voice.
Seducing me, calling me,
Leading me to the self within—
Calming, quieting the chaos—questions
Clamoring to be heard—
Crowding the peace from my soul.
The sun catches each diminutive splash
Spraying rainbows above currents of
Life-giving liquid, tumbling headlong—ever downward
Seeking out, joining others plunging towards greatness—
Home to hydrae, caddis flies, trout, otters—
Each, living its own circle.
Heedless of its gifts, the stream grows—
Changing, ever changing on its journey,
Growing in power and stature—melding with its sisters.
Separate yet inseparable—joining—
Growing stronger—giving ever more to life—
Eventually flowing into—becoming one with the sea.
Wholeness—natural completion—
My heart sings the song of life,
Its circles without endings or beginnings.
My spirit quickens to nature's ways
And I will
To learn her lessons.

Quietly,
   I sit in deep wood
      Drinking in
         The fullness of my
            Surroundings.

Crow cries—
   Magic,
      Magic,
         Magic,
            Magic . . . .
Sparrow sings—
   Joy,
      Joy . . . .
Breeze rustling leaves,
   Tickling my arm—
      Feel it . . . .

Sunlight filtering through
   Spreading branches
      Of shade tree—
Caresses me with warmth
   Feeding my spirit
      With pure energy.

I am made of Earth,
Every cell in my body—
Composed of minerals existing for eons.
I have been hunter and hunted,
Stone and vegetation.
I have been and therefore still am...
> Talons of an eagle,
> Eyes of a wolf,
> Wings of a condor,
> Heart of a lion,
> Ears of a deer,
> Nose of a hare,
> Granite of a mountain,
> Arms of an oak,
> Blades of grass. My flesh is made of all creatures,
> Mountains, and vegetation past.
The Sun is the warmth of my body—
> The fire in my veins—
> The furnace that fires Earth's molten core.
Air that fills my lungs—
> Is the substance of whale song—
> Gives loft to wings of birds—
> Is breathed by all creatures.

I am Earth in endless transmutation.
Earth is me and all else.

Her beauty
        And presence, have
No peers. As she rises,
Long slender legs unfold
        And carry her
Regal reticence from the thick
        Copse of aspen
Where she bedded this night—
        Forefoot, pause—look,
        Hind foot, pause—listen,
        Forefoot, pause—sniff,
        Hind foot, pause—nibble,
Cautiously—
        Like a predator
Stalking—lacking only
        Its intent.
She bows her head in reverence
To nibble tender new grass, then
Lifts it once more. Alert eyes—
        Glistening—
Reflecting the last vestiges of night's
        Glimmering globe—
Lacking expression, as if
        Seeing beyond 'things'.
Twitching—her nose tastes the air
For covert dangers, hidden
        In the sweetness of
A newborn day, whose breath
Wafts about—kissed by scents
        Of damp
Sage and loess.
Wishing to drink their fill—
        Her ears tip
And turn—scooping up the silence
That permeates the stillness of
        False dawn.
She lives peacefully—
Prepared, aware, yet
        Unaffected.

Golden orb of warmth and light
Hung in azure sky...
Lingering in shadows...
Icy fingers grasping at the unwary—
Last vestiges of the now closing
Time of long nights.
Mother nature preparing
Her finery for spring...
Friendly zephyrs—
Gently grooming ground and trees—
Suddenly benevolent
When driven no longer
By old man winter.
Dew drops glimmering on webs,
Strung like precious little pearls...
First steps of new-born fawns—
Tremulous, like a girl-child's
First steps in mother's heels...
Trees, bushes decked out
In lacy finery of new growth,
Accessorized with colorful splashes
Of wild flowers in myriad varieties...
Lilting melodies of songbirds—
Chatterings of squirrels and brooks—
Lifting spirits to excitement
Of renewal after hard times...
Mother nature...
Primped and poised—
Ready once again
To join the dance of life.

The wind speaks to me.
It is the voice of the Old One
Flowing through creation
Bringing comfort
On a lonely afternoon,
Sharing with me
Many secrets.
It brings to me
Scents,
Betraying the presence
Of things unseen...
      A distant fire...
      The coming of rain...
It scatters seeds—
Children of the plant people—
The hope of one more
Generation.
It carries the clouds—
Mothers bearing sacred
Waters of life—
To where the Old One ordains
Each drop must fall.
It stirs to life
Voices of the tree spirits–
Rustling leaves
Whispering stories
I long to understand.

Sly fox—
    Camouflaged—
Hidden in its surroundings...
    Ninja of the forest—
Waiting...
    For its prey.
Timid hare—
    Sniffing—
Nose a'twitch as it nibbles tender blades...
    Feeling the danger—
    Lurking unseen—
    Always present.
Within a fury 'tween predator and prey...
    Life...
            Begun and ended.
In that moment—
    When rabbit screams,
    Then forever is silenced...
Does it know of the gift it gives?
Might fox—
    In that same moment—
    Take pause...
            Giving thanks?

Seeking only solitude
          In the tranquility
                    Of a lowland meander,
Wishing to drink deeply
          Of its passive strength—
                    To learn its secret
                    Of active purpose
                              Beyond haphazard reaction . . . .
Somewhere, within the lushness
          Of early-summer green,
          Elusively teasing recollections,
                    The well-trodden path of seasons past eludes.
Perceptions gather, sharpen, seeking,
          When from above—
                    The cry of a winged voice—
                              A peregrine calls . . .
                              Feel it . . .
                                        Feel it . . . .
Suddenly, knowing is no longer
          Of bodily senses deceived
                    By illusions of preconceptions,
                              But of connectedness
                    And a voice calls . . .
                              Feel it . . .
                                        Feel it . . . .
With the eyes of my soul—
          I can share her vision.
With the ears of my spirit—
          I can hear her voice . . .
                    Feel it . . .
                              Feel it . . . .
Soaring . . .
          Soaring . . .
                    No boundaries—
          Free of perceptions
                    Influenced by reason,
I can know the strength
          Of nature's passivity—
                    Intense awareness, preparedness—
                              Without judgment or fear.
          Feel it . . .
                    Feel it . . . .

Wispy cottonwood clouds drift
    Across a lupine sky—
Giving the energy of life—
     A giant blazing star
       Rides the heavens
Looking down on a pond,
     Bounded by black birch
      And cattails
     Surrounded by wild rye-grass
      And ponderosa pines.

Seeing the shadow of an osprey
     Circling overhead,
       Brook trout dart and dive.
Bobbing on cattail perches,
     Red-winged blackbirds
      Sing their cantilenas.
Squeaking with rusty-hinge wings,
     Startled bufflehead take flight,
      Circle and disappear.

Flooding my senses
    with its beauty—
Nature restores me with
     Its patterns and parts—
      Giving refuge to my
       Weary soul.

Oval-round, hard,
　　The wood-stone
　　　　Of cherry tree
　　Whose life is yet its potential
For within,
　　Is the seed asleep—
　　　　Awaiting its destined time
To burst forth
　　The energy of life and growing,
　　　　Completing cycles
　　　　　　By bearing fruit
　　And dropping the seeds
　　　　Of the next generation.

In my life
　　I have been as a cherry stone,
　　　　Dwelling frozen and immobile,
　　Locked within a wasteland of
　　　　　　'Shoulds' and 'oughts'
But now is my time
　　For awakening,
Discovering my potential each day—
　　Stretching to the sky
　　　　Free and alive!

My Index events and dates

Order Form

Fax Orders: 1-503-543-5667

Phone Orders: 1-503-543-5323

Online Orders: wepublish@columbia-center.org

Postal Orders: Close The Loop

                              P.O. Box 748

                              Scappoose, OR 97056-0748

Please send my order to:

Name_____

Address_____

_____

_____

Total enclosed_____

Close The Loop is pleased to offer *Through My Eyes* to you directly from our warehouse. The price is $12.95. We will gladly accept your personal check. We do not accept credit card payment at this time. Our order form may be photocopied. Add $2.50 shipping & handling for each order. This product is also sold in finer book stores and gift shops. Ask your local book-seller for a copy of *Through My Eyes,* ISBN (paperback) 1-890663-00-X.